Editor
Gisela Lee, M.A.

Managing Editor
Karen Goldfluss, M.S. Ed.

Editor-in-Chief
Sharon Coan, M.S. Ed.

Illustrator
Sue Fullam

Cover Artist
Barb Lorseyedi

Art Coordinator
Kevin Barnes

Art Director
CJae Froshay

Imaging
Temo Parra
Rosa C. See

Product Manager
Phil Garcia

Publisher
Mary D. Smith, M.S. Ed.

S0-BRB-371

GRADE 5

Author

Robert W. Smith

Teacher Created Resources

Teacher Created Resources, Inc.
6421 Industry Way
Westminster, CA 92683
www.teachercreated.com

ISBN: 978-0-7439-3730-6
©2003 Teacher Created Resources, Inc.
Reprinted, 2009
Made in U.S.A.

Table of Contents

Introduction

The old adage "practice makes perfect" can really hold true for your child and his or her education. The more practice and exposure your child has with concepts being taught in school, the more success he or she is likely to find. For many parents, knowing how to help their children can be frustrating because the resources may not be readily available. As a parent it is also difficult to know where to focus your efforts so that the extra practice your child receives at home supports what he or she is learning in school.

This book has been designed to help parents and teachers reinforce basic skills with their children. *Practice Makes Perfect* reviews basic math skills for children in grade 5. The math focus is word problems. While it would be impossible to include in this book all concepts taught in grade 5, the following basic objectives are reinforced through practice exercises. These objectives support math standards established on a district, state, or national level. (Refer to the Table of Contents for the specific objectives of each practice page.)

- percentages
- adding and subtracting 2-digit numbers
- adding and subtracting 3-digit numbers
- adding and subtracting 4-digit numbers
- adding and subtracting 5- and 6-digit numbers
- multiplying numbers
- multiplying by 100 and 1,000

- tables, graphs, and charts
- choosing operations
- working with money and time
- working with fractions
- finding the average
- basic geometry

There are 36 practice pages organized sequentially so children can build their knowledge from more basic skills to higher-level math skills. To correct the practice pages in this book, use the answer key provided on pages 47 and 48. Six practice tests follow the practice pages. These provide children with multiple-choice test items to help prepare them for standardized tests administered in schools. As children complete a problem, they fill in the correct letter among the answer choices. An optional "bubble-in" answer sheet has also been provided on page 46. This answer sheet is similar to those found on standardized tests. As your child completes each test, he or she can fill in the correct bubbles on the answer sheet.

How to Make the Most of This Book

Here are some useful ideas for optimizing the practice pages in this book:

- Set aside a specific place in your home to work on the practice pages. Keep it neat and tidy with materials on hand.
- Set up a certain time of day to work on the practice pages. This will establish consistency. An alternative is to look for times in your day or week that are less hectic and more conducive to practicing skills.
- Keep all practice sessions with your child positive and constructive. If the mood becomes tense or you and your child are frustrated, set the book aside and look for another time to practice with your child.
- Help with instructions if necessary. If your child is having difficulty understanding what to do or how to get started, work the first problem through with him or her.
- Review the work your child has done. This serves as reinforcement and provides further practice.
- Allow your child to use whatever writing instruments he or she prefers. For example, colored pencils can add variety and pleasure to drill work.
- Pay attention to the areas in which your child has the most difficulty. Provide extra guidance and exercises in those areas. Allowing children to use drawings and manipulatives, such as coins, tiles, game markers, or flash cards, can help them grasp difficult concepts more easily.
- Look for ways to make real-life application to the skills being reinforced.

Practice 1 ꙮ ꙮ ꙮ ꙮ ꙮ ꙮ ꙮ ꙮ ꙮ ꙮ ꙮ ꙮ ꙮ ꙮ

Five-Step Plan
1. Read the problem carefully.
2. State the problem to be solved in your own words.
3. Determine the operation to be used.
4. Do the operation.
5. Check the answer to see if it is reasonable.

Directions: Read the following word problems. In your own words, write down what you need to find out. Then use the Five-Step Plan to solve each problem.

1. Your book has 148 pages. You have read 76 pages. How many more pages do you have to read?

   I have to find out . . . _____

   Solution: _____

2. You read 20 pages a night for 7 nights. How many pages did you read in the week?

   I have to find out . . . _____

   Solution: _____

3. You rode your bike for 40 minutes on Monday, 25 minutes on Tuesday, and 30 minutes on Wednesday. How many minutes did you ride your bike altogether?

   I have to find out . . . _____

   Solution: _____

4. You have 14 nickels, 12 dimes, and 28 pennies. How many coins do you have in all?

   I have to find out . . . _____

   Solution: _____

5. You have 16 marbles. Your best friend has 7 times as many marbles. How many marbles does your friend have?

   I have to find out . . . _____

   Solution: _____

6. A little league coach gave the team a bag of 90 hard candies to divide evenly among 10 players. How many pieces of candy did each player receive?

   I have to find out . . . _____

   Solution: _____

7. In a basketball shooting contest, you made 38 shots and your best friend made 44 shots. How many more shots did your friend make?

   I have to find out . . . _____

   Solution: _____

Practice 2

Five-Step Plan

1. Read the problem carefully.
2. State the problem to be solved in your own words.
3. Determine the operation to be used.
4. Do the operation.
5. Check the answer to see if it is reasonable.

Directions: Read the following word problems. Follow the Five-Step Plan. Write the operation you decide to use. Solve each problem.

1. There are 154 fourth graders and 173 fifth graders in Okie Dokie School. How many more fifth graders attend the school?

   Operation to Use:_____

   Solution: _____

2. It costs each student $5 a week for lunch at Okie Dokie School. How much money will be spent by 312 students buying lunch for the week?

   Operation to Use:_____

   Solution: _____

3. Each fifth grade student in Okie Dokie School has 4 textbooks in his or her desk. There are 135 fifth grade students. How many textbooks do they have altogether?

   Operation to Use:_____

   Solution: _____

4. There are 203 first graders and 198 kindergarteners at Okie Dokie School. How many students are there altogether in kindergarten and first grade?

   Operation to Use:_____

   Solution: _____

5. The Okie Dokie School cafeteria served a tray with 4 peanut butter cookies to every student who bought lunch on Monday. There were 503 students who bought lunch. How many cookies did the cafeteria serve?

   Operation to Use:_____

   Solution: _____

6. A group of 7 students won a contest and divided a bag of 161 candy bars among them. How many candy bars did each student receive?

   Operation to Use:_____

   Solution: _____

7. You can buy an Okie Dokie School kit for $4. The school sold 218 kits. How much money did it receive for the kits?

   Operation to Use:_____

   Solution: _____

Practice 3

Problem-Solving Code Words

Addition		Subtraction
altogether	change	how much older
entire cost	minus	how much taller
in all	how much less	how much saved
total	how much more	how much change
perimeter	difference	how much left
sum	how many fewer	

Directions: Using your Five-Step Plan and the Problem-Solving Code Word, find the solution to solve these problems. Underline the code words in each sentence and name the operation.

1. Your school basketball team scored 44 points in a game. Their opponents scored 29 points. How many fewer points did the other team score?

    Operation: _____ **Solution:** _____

2. There are 123 students in the 4th grade at Okie Dokie Elementary School and 149 students in the 3rd grade. How many more 3rd graders are there?

    Operation: _____ **Solution:** _____

3. The 6th grade basketball team at Okie Dokie School scored 71 points in their game against the Western Wildcats. The Wildcats scored 59 points. How many more points did the Okie Dokie 6th graders have?

    Operation: _____ **Solution:** _____

4. The coach of Okie Dokie School 6th graders bought a new basketball for $17.49. How much change did he receive from a $20 dollar bill?

    Operation: _____ **Solution:** _____

5. The school population at Okie Dokie School is 543 students. Their neighboring school has 734 students. What is the total student population of the two schools?

    Operation: _____ **Solution:** _____

6. The 6th grade at Okie Dokie School sold 674 candy boxes for a school fundraiser. The 5th grade sold 977 candy boxes. How many candy boxes did the two grades sell altogether?

    Operation: _____ **Solution:** _____

Practice 4

Problem-Solving Code Words

Multiplication	Division
times	split evenly
compute the area	divide by
find the volume	quotient
times as many	find the average
percent discount	shooting percentage
percent tax	shared
product	passing percentage
percent	passing percentage

Directions: Use your Five-Step Plan and the Problem-Solving Code Words to solve these problems. Underline the code words in each sentence and name the operation. Then find the solution.

1. Jeremy had 74 baseball trading cards. His friend, Brad, had 4 times as many trading cards. How many cards did Brad have?

   Operation: _____ **Solution:** _____

2. Allison won a huge basket containing 234 candies at a raffle. She decided to split the candies evenly among the 9 members of her girl scout troop. How many candies did each girl scout receive?

   Operation: _____ **Solution:** _____

3. The price of a haircut at Super Cool Coiffures is usually $20. Jennifer received a 10 percent discount during January. How much money did the discount save her?

   Operation: _____ **Solution:** _____

4. What is the product of 34 and 46?

   Operation: _____ **Solution:** _____

5. Divide 325 by 25. What is the quotient?

   Operation: _____ **Solution:** _____

6. There is a 10 percent tax on all clothes at the Clothes R U Department Store. What is the tax on a $90 jacket?

   Operation: _____ **Solution:** _____

7. Billy scored 23 points in a basketball game. Rebecca scored 18 points and Jose scored 19 points. Find their average score. (*Hint:* Add the scores first.)

   Operation: _____ **Solution:** _____

8. George's backyard is a rectangle 20 feet wide and 16 feet long. Compute the area.

   Operation: _____ **Solution:** _____

Practice 5 ⟳ ◉ ⟳ ◉ ⟳ ◉ ⟳ ◉ ⟳ ◉ ⟳ ◉ ⟳ ◉

Directions: Use your Five-Step Plan and the Problem-Solving Code Words to solve these problems. Underline the code words in each sentence. Name the operation and then find the solution.

1. Amy spent $97.49 on a bicycle and $35.67 on a skateboard. How much did she spend in all?

   Operation: _____ **Solution:** _____

2. Melissa listened to her favorite CD for 39 minutes and watched television for 87 minutes. How much longer did she watch television than listen to music?

   Operation: _____ **Solution:** _____

3. Shirlene's dog weighs 7 pounds. Her horse weighs 43 times as much. How many pounds does the horse weigh?

   Operation: _____ **Solution:** _____

4. Robert read 420 pages in one 5-day period. What was the average number of pages he read each day?

   Operation: _____ **Solution:** _____

5. During vacation Arthur's family drove 330 miles on Monday, 290 miles on Tuesday, and 310 miles on Wednesday. How many miles did they average each day? (*Hint:* Add the miles first.)

   Operation: _____ **Solution:** _____

6. Jeffrey has a collection of 134 baseball trading cards. Michael has a collection of 301 trading cards. How many fewer cards does Jeffrey have?

   Operation: _____ **Solution:** _____

7. Mitchell shoveled snow for 95 minutes on Tuesday and 112 minutes on Wednesday. How many minutes did he shovel snow altogether?

   Operation: _____ **Solution:** _____

8. A basketball game lasted 88 minutes. A baseball game lasted 191 minutes. How much longer was the baseball game?

   Operation: _____ **Solution:** _____

9. A team of 5 basketball players split the cost of a new basketball evenly. The ball cost $27.80. How much money did it cost each player?

   Operation: _____ **Solution:** _____

10. James got a 30 percent discount on a $100 pair of in-line skates. How much money did the discount save?

    Operation: _____ **Solution:** _____

Practice 6

Word Problem Patterns

- Problems that list several numbers or prices usually involve addition.
- Problems that compare two numbers usually involve subtraction.
- Problems that list one price or number and ask for the cost or amount of many items usually require multiplication.
- Problems that suggest splitting cost or evenly dividing amounts usually require division.

Directions: At Toys from Five to Ninety-Five, you can buy all kinds of toys and games for kids and their parents. Use the suggestions at the top of the page to help you solve some of these word problems.

1. A set of Super Balls at Toys from Five to Ninety-Five comes in a box of 12 balls. How many balls would 25 boxes hold? _____

2. Dan bought a set of jacks for $1.99, a bag of marbles for $3.39, a foam football for $4.50, and a handball for $1.25. How much money did Dan spend? _____

3. A Super-Soaker Water Pistol costs $13.79 at Toys from Five to Ninety-Five. How much change would you receive for a $20 dollar bill? _____

4. Toys from Five to Ninety-Five is selling a Racing Speed Mountain Bike for $328.79. The Basic Mountain Bike costs only $119.55. What is the difference in cost? _____

5. A deck of plastic playing cards has 52 cards. How many cards are in 300 decks?

   _____

6. A Summer Cool-Off plastic pool costs $298.44 at Toys from Five to Ninety-Five. A group of 9 neighbors decided to buy one and split the cost evenly. How much did each neighbor pay?

   _____

7. The principal bought 44 Double Tricks Yo-Yos, 261 Roller Ball marbles, 128 Super Bouncy Balls, and 77 Fly-Rite mini-planes. How many toys did he buy altogether? _____

8. Caroline bought a Super Saver bag of 170 marbles of various sizes. Suzette bought a bag of 36 marbles. How many fewer marbles did Suzette buy? _____

9. Your best friend won a contest at Toys from Five to Ninety-Five. The prize was a box with 1,440 colored marbles, which he decided to split evenly among 12 classmates. How many marbles did each classmate receive? _____

Practice 7 ꩜ ꩜ ꩜ ꩜ ꩜ ꩜ ꩜ ꩜ ꩜ ꩜

Directions: Candy Is Dandy is a candy warehouse full of sweet delights. The building is overflowing with Supersize Lollipops, Giant Chocolate Cubes, Jelly Smellies, Berry Cherry Squirters, Geodesic Gumballs, Double-Chocolate Peanut Bars, and Slurpy Suckers. Solve the following problems about the sweet delights at the candy store.

1. Candy Is Dandy has 200 bags of Supersize Lollipops. Each bag contains 25 lollipops. How many lollipops do they have? _____

2. The company has 4,048 Giant Chocolate Cubes which they intend to package in boxes of 8. How many boxes will they fill? _____

3. Candy Is Dandy has two giant tubs full of Slurpy Suckers. One tub has 2,345 Slurpy Suckers. The other has 4,199 of these candies. How many Slurpy Suckers do they have in all?

   _____

4. At the beginning of February, the company had 28,000 boxes of Heart-Shaped Chocolate Bricks. They sold 17,297 of these Chocolate Bricks in one month. How many did they have left?

   _____

5. Each box of Geodesic Gumballs contains 19 gumballs. How many gumballs are contained in 99 boxes? _____

6. In October, Candy Is Dandy sold 18,968 Halloween Geodesic Gumballs. They sold only 3,459 Geodesic Gumballs in November. How many more gumballs did they sell in October?

   _____

7. In July, the company sold 27,867 Berry Cherry Squirters. They sold 29,399 Berry Cherry Squirters in August and 19,301 in September. What were the total sales of Berry Cherry Squirters for these three months? _____

8. Double Chocolate Peanut Bars are sold in boxes of 12. The company has 7,332 bars. How many boxes will they need to package all of these bars? _____

9. Geodesic Gumballs come in buckets of 50. How many gumballs are in 300 buckets?

   _____

10. Candy Is Dandy sold 899,344 out of 1,000,000 Slurpy Suckers before Christmas. How many suckers did they have left? _____

Practice 8

Directions: Use the illustration to help you answer these questions.
Find the least common denominator (LCD) to add or subtract unlike fractions.
Reduce the fraction, if possible. The first problem is done for you.

1. How much is 1/4 plus 1/8?

$$\frac{1}{4} = \frac{2}{8}$$
$$+\frac{1}{8} = \frac{1}{8}$$

LCD = ___8___

Answer = ___$\frac{3}{8}$___

2. What is the sum of 1/3 and 1/6?

LCD = _____

Answer = _____

3. What is the difference between 1/3 and 1/6?

LCD = _____

Answer = _____

4. What is the sum of 1/6 and 1/4?

LCD = _____

Answer = _____

5. How much larger is 1/4 than 1/8?

LCD = _____

Answer = _____

6. What is the sum of 1/6 and 1/8?

LCD = _____

Answer = _____

7. What is the difference between 1/3 and 1/4?

LCD = _____

Answer = _____

8. What is the sum of 1/3 and 1/8?

LCD = _____

Answer = _____

9. How much more is 1/4 than 1/6?

LCD = _____

Answer = _____

10. Compute the difference between 1/3 and 1/8.

LCD = _____

Answer = _____

Practice 9

> **Red Hot Chili Recipe (Serves 20)**
>
> 3 lb. hamburger   4 ounces chili pepper
>
> 5 lb. beans   6 ounces hot sauce
>
> 4 lb. tomatoes   20 ounces tomato sauce
>
> 2 lb. macaroni   16 ounces water

Directions: Use the information in the recipe above to help you solve these problems. (*Hint:* Making a fraction of a recipe involves multiplication. Determining how many times a fraction fits into another number involves division.)

1. Maria wanted to make only 1/4 of the recipe. How much did she need for each ingredient?

   _____ lb. hamburger   _____ ounces chili pepper

   _____ lb. beans   _____ ounces hot sauce

   _____ lb. tomatoes   _____ ounces tomato sauce

   _____ lb. macaroni   _____ ounces water

2. Crystal wanted to make only 1/3 of the recipe. How much did she need of each ingredient?

   _____ lb. hamburger   _____ ounces chili pepper

   _____ lb. beans   _____ ounces hot sauce

   _____ lb. tomatoes   _____ ounces tomato sauce

   _____ lb. macaroni   _____ ounces water

3. Patti made exactly 1/2 of the recipe. How much did she need of each ingredient?

   _____ lb.hamburger   _____ ounces chili pepper

   _____ lb. beans   _____ ounces hot sauce

   _____ lb. tomatoes   _____ ounces tomato sauce

   _____ lb. macaroni   _____ ounces water

4. Chili beans came in 1/2 lb. bags. How many bags of chili beans would Julie need to make the original recipe? _____

5. Tomatoes can be purchased in 3/4 lb. sacks. How many sacks of tomatoes would Julie need to make the original recipe? _____

6. Macaroni can be bought in 2/3 lb. boxes. How many boxes of macaroni would Julie need to make the original recipe? _____

7. Hamburger can be bought in 1/2 lb. trays. How many trays of hamburger would Julie need to make the original recipe? _____

Practice 10

Directions: The fifth grade at Garfield Elementary School is growing a garden as a class science project. They are keeping a careful record of exactly how much water they are using for each plant. Help the class solve these word problems.

1. Doreen poured 1/4 of a quart of water near each corn plant. How much water did she give to all 20 corn plants? _____

2. James gave 1/3 of a quart of water to the marigold and one whole quart to the sunflower. How much more water did he give to the sunflower? _____

3. Allison divided 7/8 of a gallon of water evenly among the 14 green bean plants. How much water did she use for each plant? _____

4. Melissa split 2/3 of a gallon of water evenly among 6 pumpkin plants. How much water did she distribute to each pumpkin plant? _____

5. George used 2/3 of a quart of water for each of 30 cherry tomatoes. How much water did he use for all 30 cherry tomato plants? _____

6. Eleanor gave 5/12 of a quart of water to a squash plant and 1/3 of a quart to a cucumber plant. How much more water did she give to the squash plant? _____

7. Frank split 5/6 of a quart of water evenly among his 15 radishes. How much water did he give to each radish? _____

8. Corine gave 5/12 of a quart of water to her pole bean plant and 3/8 of a quart to her lima bean plant. How much water did she use for both plants? _____

9. Robert divided 2 full gallons of water by giving each of his sweet peas 1/9 of a gallon. How many sweet peas did he water? _____

10. Elaine used 11/12 of a gallon of water on her plants. Amanda used 5/6 of a gallon on her plants. How much less water did Amanda use? _____

Practice 11 ⟳ ⟲ ⟳ ⟲ ⟳ ⟲ ⟳ ⟲ ⟳ ⟲ ⟳ ⟲ ⟳ ⟲

Directions: Insects come in many lengths. Some of them are much smaller than an inch. Solve these insect word problems.

1. A house fly is 1/8 inches long. A vinegar fly is 1/16 inches long. How much longer is the house fly? _____

2. The blue bottle fly is 1/2 inches long. The biting stable fly is 3/8 inches long. What is their combined length? _____

3. The screw-worm fly is 5/8 inches long. The bee killer fly is 3/4 inches long. How much longer is the bee killer? _____

4. The two-spotted ladybug beetle is 1/4 inches long. How many of these beetles would be in a line $4\frac{1}{2}$ inches long? _____

5. The locust borer is 3/4 inches long. How long would a line of 16 locust borers be?

   _____

6. The stored-grain billbug is 1/8 inches long. How many billbugs would be in a line $7\frac{3}{4}$ inches long? _____

7. The snow flea is 1/16 inches long. The six-spotted green tiger beetle is 5/8 inches long. How much shorter is the snow flea? _____

8. What is the combined length of a 5/8 inches long, large milkweed bug and a 1/2 inches small milkweed bug? _____

9. How many 1/4 inches long boll weevils would fit in a line $9\frac{3}{4}$ inches long?

   _____

10. The yellow mealworm beetle is $1\frac{3}{5}$ inches long. How long of a line would 32 beetles make?

    _____

Practice 12 ⟲ ⟲ ⟲ ⟲ ⟲ ⟲ ⟲ ⟲ ⟲ ⟲ ⟲ ⟲ ⟲ ⟲

Directions: Use the illustration of a ruler to help you answer these questions. Remember to find the common denominator. The first one is done for you.

1. What is the sum of $1\frac{1}{2}$ inches and $2\frac{1}{4}$ inches? _____

2. What is the sum of $3\frac{1}{2}$ inches and $1\frac{1}{4}$ inches? _____

3. What is the difference between $3\frac{1}{4}$ inches and $2\frac{1}{2}$ inches? _____

4. How much more than 2 inches is $3\frac{1}{2}$ inches? _____

5. What is the total length of $2\frac{1}{8}$ inches and $3\frac{1}{2}$ inches? _____

6. How much shorter than 7 inches is $4\frac{1}{4}$ inches? _____

7. What is the total length of $3\frac{7}{8}$ inches and $2\frac{3}{4}$ inches? _____

8. What is the difference in length between $5\frac{3}{4}$ inches and $2\frac{7}{8}$ inches? _____

9. Compute the sum of $3\frac{5}{8}$ inches and $6\frac{1}{2}$ inches _____

10. Compute the sum of $3\frac{1}{2}$ inches, $2\frac{1}{4}$ inches, and 3 inches _____

$\frac{1}{8}$ $\frac{1}{4}$ $\frac{1}{2}$

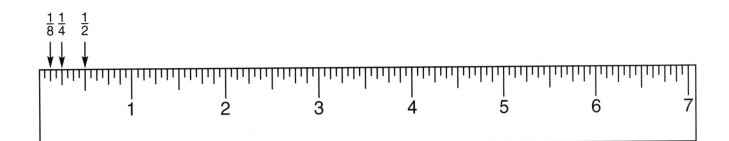

Practice 13 ꙮ ꙮ ꙮ ꙮ ꙮ ꙮ ꙮ ꙮ ꙮ ꙮ ꙮ ꙮ ꙮ ꙮ ꙮ

Directions: Garfield School decided to hold a bike-a-thon to raise money for the PTA. Many students participated and rode their bicycles along a neighborhood route. Help students determine their speeds and distances in these word problems.

Helpful Hints

- Multiply if you know the distance for one minute and need to find the distance for several minutes.

- Divide if you know the time for several blocks and need to find the time for one block.

---

1. Jimmy rode his bike 1/10 of a mile in one minute. How far could he ride in 15 minutes?

   _____

2. Veronica rode $18\frac{3}{4}$ blocks in $12\frac{1}{2}$ minutes. How many minutes did it take her to ride one block?

   _____

3. Alexander rode his bike 1/8 of a mile in one minute. How far could he ride his bike in 10 2/3

   minutes? _____

4. Allen rode his mountain bike $2\frac{1}{2}$ blocks in one minute. How many minutes would it take him to

   ride 20 blocks? _____

5. Joseph was able to ride his ten-speed racer $24\frac{1}{2}$ blocks in $10\frac{1}{2}$ minutes. How long did it take him

   to ride each block? _____

6. Jeffrey rode his dad's old beach cruiser bicycle $3\frac{1}{2}$ miles in one hour. How many miles could he

   cover in $2\frac{1}{2}$ hours? _____

7. Patti rode 22 blocks in $29\frac{1}{3}$ minutes. How many blocks could she ride in one minute?

   _____

8. Christie rode 24 blocks in one hour. How many blocks could she ride in $2\frac{1}{4}$ hours?

   _____

9. Kristin rode $16\frac{1}{2}$ blocks in 33 minutes. How many blocks did she ride in one minute?

   _____

10. Matthew rode 1/9 of a mile in one minute. How far could he ride in $22\frac{1}{2}$ minutes?

   _____

Practice 14 ❧ ❧ ❧ ❧ ❧ ❧ ❧ ❧ ❧ ❧ ❧ ❧ ❧ ❧

Directions: The school science fair is filled with all kinds of exhibits and experiments. There are wires, bulbs, chemicals, plants, and animals. Solve these word problems for the students.

1. Jeffrey used $23\frac{1}{2}$ inches of wire on his electromagnet and $4\frac{1}{3}$ inches to connect it to his battery. How much wire did he use altogether? _____

2. Crystal used $3\frac{1}{3}$ ounces of vinegar in the first trial of her mini-rocket and $4\frac{4}{5}$ ounces on the second trial. How much more vinegar did she use on the second trial?

   _____

3. Allison used $3\frac{1}{2}$ ounces of baking soda divided evenly among 7 bubbling experiments. How much did she use in each experiment? _____

4. Irene used $4\frac{1}{2}$ inches of wire for each connection on her circuit. How much wire did she use for all 8 connections? _____

5. Doreen had a roll with 10 feet of wire to use for her motor. She used $7\frac{5}{8}$ feet How much wire was left? _____

6. Anthony compared the growth of two bean stalks. The first was $11\frac{1}{2}$ inches tall. The second one was $10\frac{1}{3}$ inches tall. How much taller was the first stalk?

   _____

7. Erica compared the weights of two rats. The first rat weighed 17 ounces The second rat weighed $9\frac{11}{16}$ ounces How much less did the second rat weigh? _____

8. The length of Jessica's model parachute was $2\frac{3}{4}$ feet. It was divided evenly into 11 folds. How long was each fold? _____

9. Erik used $2\frac{1}{2}$ ounces of water for his mini-tornado model. He used 8 times as much water in his larger model. How much water did he use for the larger model?

   _____

10. The third graders used $3\frac{1}{2}$ gallons of water in their experiments. The fourth graders used $5\frac{1}{3}$ times as much water. How much water did the fourth graders use?

    _____

Practice 15 ⟅ ⟐ ⟐ ⟐ ⟐ ⟐ ⟐ ⟐ ⟐ ⟐ ⟐ ⟐ ⟐ ⟐ ⟐ ⟐ ⟐

Directions: "Spider" Brown has an immense collection of his favorite creatures—spiders. He has dozens of species and is always happy to find new additions to his collection. Help him organize his collection by doing these word problems.

1. Spider has a $2\frac{1}{2}$ inches long male desert tarantula. He also has a $2\frac{3}{4}$ inches long female. How much longer is the female? _____

2. He has one male Californian trapdoor spider which is 3/4 inches long and a female which is $1\frac{1}{8}$ inches long. How much shorter is the male? _____

3. Spider's collection includes a line of 18 female violin spiders. Each one is 3/8 inches long. How long is the line? _____

4. Each leg of a six-spotted fishing spider is $2\frac{1}{2}$ inches What is the length of all 8 legs?

   _____

5. Each leg of a brownish-gray fishing spider is $3\frac{1}{16}$ inches How much shorter is the $2\frac{1}{2}$ inches leg of the six-spotted fishing spider? _____

6. Spider's collection shows a line of 24 female Carolina wolf spiders. Each spider is $1\frac{3}{8}$ inches long. How long is the line? _____

7. Spider has one giant, desert hairy scorpion which is $5\frac{1}{2}$ inches long. He can fit 11 male rabid wolf spiders next to the scorpion. How long is each wolf spider?

   _____

8. Spider has a line of American house spiders which is $8\frac{3}{4}$ inches long. Each spider is 1/8 inches long. How many American house spiders are in the line?

   _____

9. Spider has 10 male barn spiders in a line. Each barn spider is 3/4 inches long. How long is the line? _____

10. A spider mite is 1/64 of an inch long. A female desert tarantula is $2\frac{3}{4}$ inches long. How much longer is the tarantula? _____

Practice 16 ෧ ෧ ෧ ෧ ෧ ෧ ෧ ෧ ෧ ෧ ෧ ෧ ෧ ෧ ෧

Directions: Use your skills to solve these word problems.

Note: The Anywhere House has a huge selection of CDs featuring the most popular music today. All answers involving money must have a dollar sign and a decimal point.

1. The latest CD from Jake and the Jellyfish usually sells for $14.98, but The Anywhere House has it on sale for $11.88. How much will you save by buying it at The Anywhere House?

   _____

2. A new pop singer named Dandy Sandy has released a CD which sells for $6.99. The Anywhere House sold 30 of these CDs the first day it was released. How much money did the store receive for the 30 CD's? _____

3. The newest release from The Grateful Ghosts is sold in most stores for $14.99, but The Anywhere House has priced it at $9.27. How much would you save on that CD at The Anywhere House?

   _____

4. Hill Billy Hank's latest CD *Welfare Line for Love* brought in $369.00 on its release date at The Anywhere House, which was selling it for $9 each. How many CDs did they sell on the release date? _____

5. Hill Billy and Wailing Willie released a CD of their duets which sold for $11.96. The Anywhere House sold 50 of their duet CDs in one day. How much money did they collect for these CDs?

   _____

6. You bought a CD for $11.96 and one for $6.99. What is the total cost? _____

7. The cost of a duet CD by Hill Billy and Wailing Willie is $11.96. A duet by Lord Larry and Queen Kathy costs $19.08. How much more is the Lord Larry and Queen Kathy CD?

   _____

8. The Anywhere House sold 97 CDs at $11.96 each on one day. How much money did they receive for all these CDs? _____

9. The Anywhere House sold 203 CDs at a special price of $6.99. How much money did they collect for all these CDs? _____

10. They sold 25 CDs for $477.00. What was the cost of each of these CDs? _____

Practice 17 ꙮ ꙮ ꙮ ꙮ ꙮ ꙮ ꙮ ꙮ ꙮ ꙮ ꙮ ꙮ ꙮ

Forty-one Flavors is a popular new ice-cream parlor. Here are some of their prices.

Price List

single scoop	$0.99	regular sundae	$2.50
double scoop	$1.49	large sundae	$3.25
triple scoop	$1.95	super sundae	$4.00
quadruple scoop	$2.39	cola float	$3.50

Directions: Use your skills to solve these word problems.

Remember: All answers involving money must have a dollar sign and a decimal point.

1. Your best friend bought a triple scoop of blackberry ice cream. How much more did it cost than a double scoop? _____

2. The best player on the school basketball team bought a large sundae and a triple scoop of plum nuts ice cream. How much did the player spend altogether? _____

3. The basketball coach bought a regular sundae for all 12 of her players. What was the cost of the 12 sundaes? _____

4. The soccer coach spent $56 on super sundaes. How many super sundaes did she buy? _____

5. Your mother paid for a quadruple scoop, a triple scoop, and a double scoop for you and your friends. What was the total cost? _____

6. A third grade teacher bought each of her 20 students a double scoop of ice cream. How much did it cost the teacher? _____

7. Your best friend's mother spent $65 on large sundaes for a birthday party. How many large sundaes did she buy? _____

8. Elaine bought a single scoop, Darlene bought a double scoop, and Jordan bought a quadruple scoop of black 'n blueberry ice cream. How much did they spend in all? _____

9. A Girl Scout® troop leader bought 18 cola floats for her scouts. How much did she spend? _____

10. How much more does it cost for a quadruple scoop than for a double scoop of ice cream? _____

Practice 18 ꙮ ꙮ ꙮ ꙮ ꙮ ꙮ ꙮ ꙮ ꙮ ꙮ ꙮ ꙮ ꙮ ꙮ ꙮ

The Holey Doughnut is a sweet success. The owner has invented several new types of doughnuts. Help him figure out how much each customer owes.

Price List			
Creamy Dream	$1.99	Doggy Doughnut	$2.49
Juicy Jelly	$2.25	Plum Nuts Filled	$1.75
Tiger Twist	$1.49	Round Mound	$2.99

Directions: Use your mathematics skills to solve these word problems.
Remember: All answers involving money have a dollar sign and decimal point.

1. Your best friend bought a Doggy Doughnut and a Plum Nuts Filled for his breakfast. How much did it cost him? _____

2. How much less does it cost for a Plum Nuts Filled than for a Round Mound?

   _____

3. You bought a Tiger Twist. How much change did you get for a $10 bill? _____

4. A group of 6 teenagers spent $24.60. They split the cost evenly. How much money should each teenager pay? _____

5. Your coach bought a Creamy Dream, a Juicy Jelly, and a Round Mound. How much did he spend? _____

6. A grandfather bought each of his 9 grandchildren a Plum Nuts Filled. How much did it cost him?

   _____

7. The fifth grade teacher bought 30 Juicy Jelly doughnuts for her class. How much did it cost her?

   _____

8. The girls' soccer coach bought 15 Round Mounds for her team. How much did she pay?

   _____

9. A group of 20 teenagers bought $98.80 worth of doughnuts and split the cost evenly among them. How much did each teenager pay? _____

10. Mike bought one of each doughnut. How much did Mike spend? _____

Practice 19 ⟿ ⟿ ⟿ ⟿ ⟿ ⟿ ⟿ ⟿ ⟿ ⟿ ⟿ ⟿ ⟿ ⟿

You can rent any movie title at Video Bonanza, which has the latest releases and old favorites, as well as classic movies.

Rental Prices			
just released	$3.99	old favorite	$2.99
recent movie	$3.50	classic	$2.50
music video	$3.25		

Directions: Use your skills to solve these word problems.

Remember: All answers involving money must have a dollar sign and a decimal point.

1. Your mother gave a video party for you and your friends. She rented 7 old favorites for you to choose from. How much did she spend? _____

2. As a class reward, your teacher rented the just released video entitled *Cheerleaders Play Football*. How much change did the teacher receive from a $20 dollar bill? _____

3. You and your friends decide to spend Friday evening watching a series of 5 horror flicks. How much does it cost to rent the 5 old favorites? _____

4. A group of girls in your class have a sleepover. One mother rents 9 music videos to match each girl's taste in music. How much did it cost to rent the videos? _____

5. The soccer coach rented a series of soccer movies, including 1 just released, 1 recent movie, 1 old favorite, and 1 classic. How much did the coach spend on rental fees? _____

6. A group of 7 friends spent $28.70 on video fees. They split the cost evenly. How much did each friend pay? _____

7. The school's music teacher rented 1 old favorite, 1 classic, and 1 music video for her class. How much did she spend? _____

8. The football coach rented 1 just released movie. How much change did he get from a $10 bill? _____

9. The principal spent $14.95 on rental fees. How much change did he get from a $100 bill? _____

10. Your best friend's mother rented 2 old favorites and 3 just released movies for a birthday celebration. How much did it cost her? _____

Practice 20 ❧ ❧ ❧ ❧ ❧ ❧ ❧ ❧ ❧ ❧ ❧ ❧ ❧ ❧ ❧

Directions: Use your knowledge of decimals to help you solve these problems.

1. The Texas-horned lizard is 18.1 centimeters long. The short-horned lizard is 14.5 centimeters long. How much longer is the Texas horned lizard?

   _____

2. A western-fence lizard is 23.5 centimeters long. A fringe-toed lizard is 17.9 centimeters long. How much shorter is the fringe-toed lizard? _____

3. One black-tailed rattlesnake is 70.99 centimeters long. A second black-tailed rattlesnake is 124.97 centimeters long. What is their combined length?

   _____

4. A western skunk is 23.7 centimeters long. A racer snake is 195.5 centimeters long. How much longer is the snake? _____

5. A common kingsnake is 208.3 centimeters long. A prairie kingsnake is 132.24 centimeters long. What would be the length of the two snakes if they were stretched end to end? _____

6. A Louisiana milk snake is 78.9 centimeters long. A Mexican milk snake is 99 centimeters long. What is the total length of the two snakes?

   _____

7. A western rattlesnake is 162.6 centimeters long. A tiger rattlesnake is 91.39 centimeters long. How much shorter is the tiger rattlesnake? _____

8. What is the combined length of a cottonmouth 189.2 centimeters long, a timber rattlesnake 88.9 centimeters long, and a lined snake 53.3 centimeters long?

   _____

9. A chuckwalla is 41.9 centimeters long. A banded gecko is 14.99 centimeters long. What is the difference in lengths? _____

10. What is the combined length of a sidewinder that is 82.39 centimeters long, a diamondback rattlesnake that is 212.99 centimeters long, and a copperhead that is 134.83 centimeters long? _____

Practice 21 ꙮ ꙮ ꙮ ꙮ ꙮ ꙮ ꙮ ꙮ ꙮ ꙮ ꙮ ꙮ ꙮ

Directions: Birds have hollow bones which help keep them light. Use your knowledge of decimals to help you solve these problems.

1. A California quail weighs 0.180 kilograms. How much would 3 California quail weigh? _____

2. A sky lark weighs 1.4 ounces. How much would 20 sky larks weigh?
_____

3. A mallard duck weighs 2.4 pounds. How much would 12 mallard ducks weigh?
_____

4. A snow goose weighs 7.4 pounds. What is the weight of 15 snow geese?
_____

5. A green heron weighs 0.87 kilograms. What is the weight of 30 green herons?
_____

6. The golden eagle weighs 4.575 kilograms. What is the weight of 21 golden eagles?
_____

7. A crow weighs 0.45 kilograms. What is the weight of 100 crows? _____

8. A robin weighs 0.077 kilograms. What is the weight of 40 robins? _____

9. A hummingbird weighs 0.11 ounces. How much do 50 hummingbirds weigh?
_____

10. The great horned owl weighs 3.1 pounds. What is the weight of 25 great horned owls?
_____

 #3730 Practice Makes Perfect: Word Problems

Practice 22 ⟋ ⟋ ⟋ ⟋ ⟋ ⟋ ⟋ ⟋ ⟋ ⟋ ⟋ ⟋

Directions: Dr. Dooley D. Vision is known as "The Great Divider." He is very famous for his ability to divide things fairly and evenly. He is often hired by families and companies to avoid disputes. Help him do the problems below.

1. Dr. D. Vision has a stick of licorice 105.25 meters long. He intends to split it evenly among 5 of his nephews. How much licorice will each nephew receive? _____

2. The Forty-One Flavors ice cream store asked Dr. Vision to help a teacher divide 108.4 ounces of ice cream among her 20 students. How many ounces of ice cream did each child receive?

   _____

3. Dr. D. Vision decided to divide the money in his piggy bank among 7 of his grandchildren. He had $122.01. How much money did each grandchild receive? _____

4. The Candy Is Dandy factory hired Dr. D. Vision to help them divide 340.8 ounces of chocolate among 80 chocolate bars. How much chocolate was in each bar? _____

5. Dr. D. Vision helped the school custodian cut a 183.6 foot rope into 9 even jump ropes. How long was each jump rope? _____

6. Dr. Vision was hired to make sure that everyone at a party got the same amount of cake. The cake weighed 107.75 ounces and there were 25 guests. How much cake did each guest receive?

   _____

7. Dr. D. Vision was hired to place 10 markers at even intervals along a public road which was 563.9 feet long. How long was each interval? _____

8. Dooley had a bag with 18.81 grams of gold dust which he intended to split evenly among his 9 favorite neighbors. How much gold dust did each neighbor receive? _____

9. The Great Divider was hired to divide a vat of 896.4 ounces of chocolate fudge into 90 jars. How much fudge went into each jar? _____

10. Dooley marked a 88.78 mile long state highway into 100 even sections. How long was each section? _____

11. Dr. D. Vision divided 678.223 ounces of sugar among 1,000 candy bars. How much sugar went into each candy bar? _____

Practice 23 ᕙ ᕗ ᕙ ᕗ ᕙ ᕗ ᕙ ᕗ ᕙ ᕗ ᕙ ᕗ ᕙ ᕗ ᕙ ᕗ

Directions: This bar graph illustrates the votes some states will have in the Electoral College in the year 2004. The Electoral College casts 538 votes to determine the next President of the United States. A majority of 270 votes are needed to winches Study the graph and answer these questions.

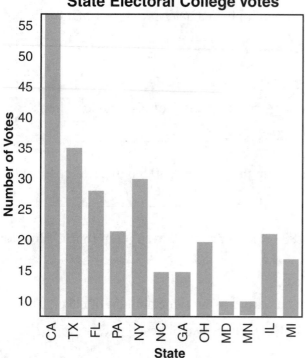

State Electoral College Votes

1. Which state has the most votes in the Electoral College? _____

2. Which two states have exactly 10 votes in the Electoral College? _____

3. Which two states have 21 votes in the Electoral College? _____

4. Which state has 17 votes in the Electoral College? _____

5. How many votes does North Carolina have? _____

6. How many votes does Ohio have? _____

7. Which state has 10 more votes than Illinois? _____

Directions: This double bar graph illustrates the results of a student questionnaire about the average amount of time spent weekly on homework and watching television. Study the graph and answer these questions.

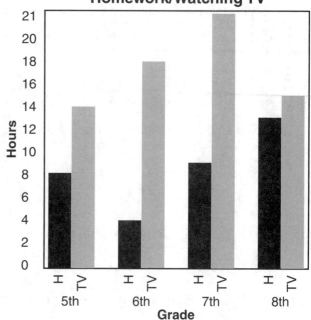

Average Time Spent on Homework/Watching TV

8. Which grade averaged 8 hours a week of homework and 14 hours of television watching? _____

9. Which grade watched the most television? _____

10. Which grade did the most homework in one week? _____

11. Which grade did only 4 hours of homework? _____

12. Which grade spent almost as much time on homework as on watching television? _____

13. Which grade spent 14 more hours watching television than they did on homework? _____

14. Which grade spent 21 hours a week watching television? _____

Practice 24 ⟲ ⟲ ⟲ ⟲ ⟲ ⟲ ⟲ ⟲ ⟲ ⟲ ⟲ ⟲ ⟲ ⟲ ⟲

Directions: A line graph illustrates change over time. This graph illustrates human life expectancies at times from 400 B.C. in Greece to A.D. 2000 in the United States. Use the graph to answer these questions.

Estimated Life Expectancy

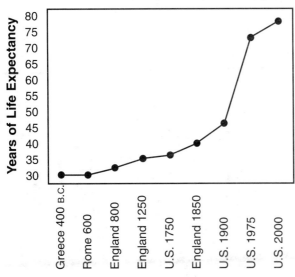

1. What was the life expectancy in England about the year 1250? _____

2. What was the average age a person lived to in Greece in the year 400 B.C.? _____

3. In what country and year was the life expectancy 47 years? _____

4. What is the difference in average life expectancy from Greece in 400 B.C. to the United States in 2000? _____

5. In what year in the United States was the life expectancy 36 years? _____

6. In what century did life expectancy increase 30 years? _____

7. How many years did it take for life expectancy to increase from 30 years in Greece to 40 years in England?
   _____

Directions: The double line graph shows the number of home runs hit by the home run leader in each league for a 10-year period. Study the graph and answer these questions.

Annual Home Runs

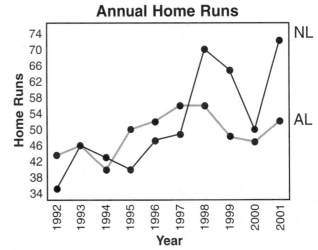

8. In which year were the most home runs hit by one batter? _____

9. In which year did the American League (AL) leader and the National League (NL) leader hit the same number of home runs?
   _____

10. In which two years did the American League leader hit 56 home runs?
    _____

11. In what year did the American League leader hit only 40 home runs? _____

12. In which year were the fewest total home runs hit by the leaders in the two leagues?
    _____

13. In which five years did the National League leader hit more home runs than the American League leader? _____
    _____

14. In which four years did the American League leader hit more home runs than the National League leader? _____
    _____

15. Which league's leaders hit more home runs over the 10 year period? _____

Practice 25

Directions: This pictograph represents a survey of sports preferences among grade school students in the 4th through 6th grades. Study the pictograph and answer the questions below.

Students' Favorite Sports

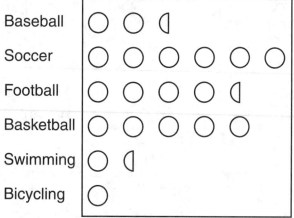

Key: O = 10 students

Directions: This line plot illustrates the number of books read by individual students in one month. Each x stands for one student and the number of books that they read. Study the line plot and answer the questions.

Survey of Student Readers Line Plot

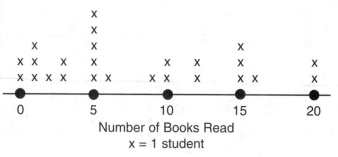

Number of Books Read
x = 1 student

1. How many students prefer to play basketball? _____

2. How many students prefer bicycling as their favorite sport? _____

3. How many students prefer to play baseball? _____

4. How many students prefer football as their favorite sport? _____

5. Which are the two most favorite sports? _____ _____

6. Which are the two least favorite sports? _____ _____

7. How many more students prefer soccer than to swimming? _____

8. How many more students prefer football compared to baseball? _____

9. What is the total number of students surveyed? _____

10. How many students read 20 books in one month? _____

11. How many students read no books in the month? _____

12. Did any students read exactly 16 books? _____

13. How many students read 12 books? _____

14. How many students read 15 books in one month? _____

15. What is the total number of students who read less than 5 books? _____

16. What is the total number of books read by all the students in the survey? _____

Practice 26 ꒰ ꒰ ꒰ ꒰ ꒰ ꒰ ꒰ ꒰ ꒰ ꒰ ꒰ ꒰ ꒰ ꒰ ꒰ ꒰

Directions: The following frequency table records the responses of fifth graders when asked to name their favorite table game. Study the table and answer the questions below.

Game	Tally	Frequency
Checkers	ⅣⅢ ⅣⅢ ///	13
Chess	ⅣⅢ //	7
Twenty-One	////	4
War	ⅣⅢ ////	9
Hearts	//	2
Old Maid	/	1
Chinese Checkers	///	3
Solitaire	////	4
None	ⅣⅢ /	6

1. Which was the most favorite table game? _____

2. Which was the least favorite table game? _____

3. How many 5th graders liked no table game? _____

4. How many more 5th graders preferred Chess to Old Maid? _____

5. How many more students liked Checkers better than Chess? _____

6. Which two card games were preferred by 4 students? _____

7. How many students participated in the survey? _____

8. What is the total number of students that preferred the board games: Chess, Checkers, and Chinese Checkers? _____

Directions: This chart lists the wingspan (from the tip of one wing to the tip of the other wing) of some birds. Study the chart and answer the questions below.

turkey vulture	72 inches	golden eagle	92 inches
black vulture	60 inches	bald eagle	96 inches
red-tailed hawk	54 inches	red-shouldered hawk	48 inches
sparrow hawk	23 inches		

9. What is the wingspan of the sparrow hawk? _____

10. What is the wingspan of the black vulture? _____

11. Which bird on the chart has the widest wingspan? _____

12. Which bird on the chart has the shortest wingspan? _____

13. How much longer is the wingspan of the bald eagle than the wingspan of the turkey vulture? _____

14. What is the difference between the wingspans of the red-tailed hawk and the black vulture? _____

Practice 27

The Lawn Magicians is a business run by three fifth grade friends. They will mow and edge any lawn in the neighborhood for a very reasonable fee.

Directions: Compute the perimeter of each lawn in the problems below

Remember: The perimeter is the distance around a geometric figure.

1. The Lawn Magicians got a job edging a rectangular lawn which is 12 feet long and 7 feet wide. What is the perimeter of this lawn? _____

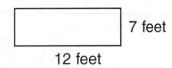

7 feet

12 feet

2. One neighbor had a lawn shaped like a pentagon. Each side was 9 feet long. What is the perimeter? _____

9 feet

3. Mr. Cranky's lawn was shaped like a parallelogram. The shorter sides were 8 meters long and the longer sides were 18 meters long. What is the perimeter?

_____

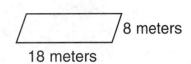

8 meters

18 meters

4. Doctor Cutter's lawn was a trapezoid with these lengths: 9 meters, 12 meters, 10 meters, and 17 meters. What is the perimeter of his lawn? _____

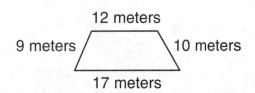

12 meters

9 meters   10 meters

17 meters

5. The local dentist had a lawn shaped like an isosceles triangle with two sides which were 8 meters long and a base of 5 meters. What is the distance around this lawn?

_____

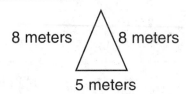

8 meters   8 meters

5 meters

6. The Lawn Magicians edged a lawn with five sides. These were the lengths of each side: 9 meters, 7 meters, 6 meters, 12 meters, and 6 meters. What is the perimeter of this lawn? _____

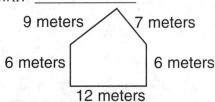

9 meters   7 meters

6 meters   6 meters

12 meters

7. Mrs. Rose's lawn had five sides with these lengths: 8 feet, 7 feet, 12 feet, 6 feet, and 10 feet. What was the distance around this lawn? _____

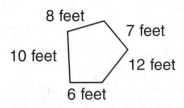

8 feet

7 feet

10 feet

12 feet

6 feet

8. Mr. Octo had a lawn with 8 sides. Each side was 7 meters long. What is the perimeter?

_____

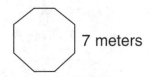

7 meters

Practice 28 ✺ ✺ ✺ ✺ ✺ ✺ ✺ ✺ ✺ ✺ ✺ ✺ ✺ ✺

The Lawn Magicians are three fifth grade friends who earn money mowing their neighbors' lawns. They charge by the square foot so they have to know the area of each lawn they mow.

Directions: Help the Lawn Magicians compute the area of each lawn described below.

Remember These Formulas: Area of a rectangle = base times height; Area of a parallelogram = base times height; Area of a triangle = base times height divided by 2

1. Mr. Steven's yard is a parallelogram 9 feet high and 15 feet at the base. What is the area of his lawn? _____

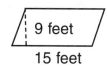
9 feet
15 feet

2. Mrs. Frank's rectangular lawn measures 12 feet by 6 feet. How many square feet does it cover? _____

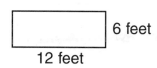
6 feet
12 feet

3. Mr. Ellis's lawn is shaped like an isosceles triangle. It has a height of 8 feet and a 6 feet base. What is the area of his lawn?

_____

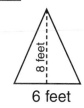
8 feet
6 feet

4. Mrs. Sharp's lawn is a triangle with a height of 16 feet and a base of 17 feet. How many square feet will the Lawn Magicians mow?

_____

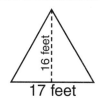
16 feet
17 feet

5. The Lawn Magicians mowed their next door neighbor's rectangular lawn which was 8 feet by 24 feet What was the area in square feet? _____

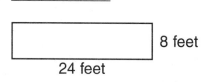
8 feet
24 feet

6. Mr. Potter's lawn was a parallelogram 8 feet high and 9 feet at the base. How many square feet did the lawn cover?

_____

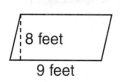
8 feet
9 feet

7. Ms. Breen's lawn was shaped like a parallelogram with a height of 16 feet and a base of 20 feet. What was the area in square feet? _____

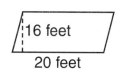
16 feet
20 feet

8. Mrs. Ricardo's lawn was square. It was 13 feet on each side. How many square feet did the Lawn Magicians have to mow?

_____

13 feet

Practice 29

Directions: A straight angle has 180 degrees. A right angle has 90 degrees. An angle may face in any direction. Determine the number of degrees in each angle labeled *x*.

1.

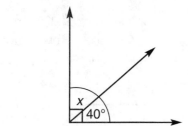

5.

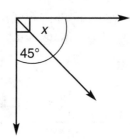

2.

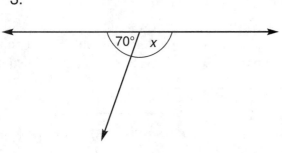

6.

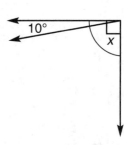

3.

7.

4.

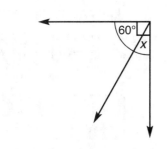

8.

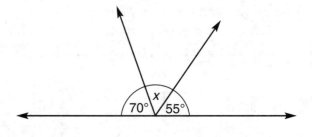

Practice 30

Directions: The three interior angles of a triangle always total 180 degrees. A right angle always has 90 degrees. A triangle with three equal sides has three equal angles—each 60 degrees. Angles opposite equal sides are equal. Determine the number of degrees in each angle labeled *x*.

1. *x* = _____

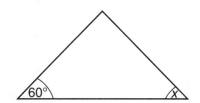

5. *x* = _____

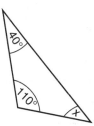

2. *x* = _____

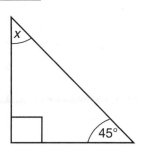

6. *x* = _____

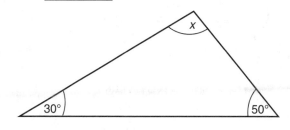

3. *x* = _____

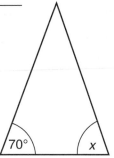

7. *x* = _____

4. *x* = _____

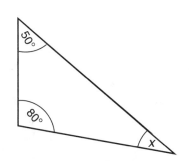

8. *x* = _____

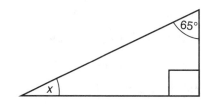

Practice 31 ꩜ ꩜ ꩜ ꩜ ꩜ ꩜ ꩜ ꩜ ꩜ ꩜ ꩜ ꩜ ꩜ ꩜ ꩜

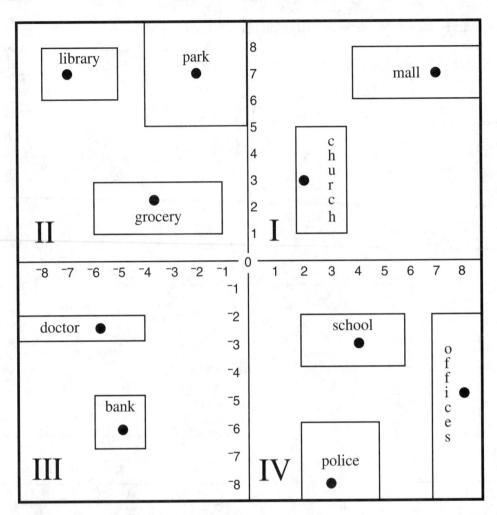

Directions: Study the city grid shown above. Notice where landmarks such as the bank and park are located. Notice which numbers are positive and which are negative. Note how the four quadrants are labeled: I, II, III, and IV. Use the information to answer these word problems. **Remember:** Always go across before going up or down and use the point for finding the coordinate.

1. What feature is located at coordinates (7, 7)? _____

2. What building is located at coordinates (4, ⁻3)? _____

3. Which business is located at (⁻5, ⁻6)? _____

4. Which quadrant has all negative numbers? _____

5. Which quadrant has only positive coordinates? _____

6. What are the coordinates of the police station? _____

7. Which public building is located at coordinates (⁻7, 7)? _____

8. What are the coordinates of the church? _____

9. What public area is located at coordinates (⁻2, 7)? _____

10. Which quadrant always begins with a positive number and concludes with a negative number?
    _____

Practice 32 ꩜ ꩜ ꩜ ꩜ ꩜ ꩜ ꩜ ꩜ ꩜ ꩜ ꩜ ꩜ ꩜ ꩜

Equations can often be written to make problem solving easier.

• What number is 4 less than 7?

$n = 7 - 4$ so $n = 3$

• What number less 11 is 18?

$n - 11 = 18$ so $n = 29$

Directions: Write an equation for each word problem. Then solve the equation. The first one is done for you.

1. What number is 7 less than 20?

   Equation: ___$n = 20 - 7$___

   Solution: ___$n = 13$___

2. What number is 13 less than 30?

   Equation: _____

   Solution: _____

3. What number added to 9 equals 15?

   Equation: _____

   Solution: _____

4. What number is 4 more than 29?

   Equation: _____

   Solution: _____

5. What number less 14 is 29?

   Equation: _____

   Solution: _____

6. What number plus 23 equals 30?

   Equation: _____

   Solution: _____

7. What number added to 22 equals 40?

   Equation: _____

   Solution: _____

8. What number is 22 less than 60?

   Equation: _____

   Solution: _____

9. What number added to 25 equals 61?

   Equation: _____

   Solution: _____

10. What number added to 16 equals 40 plus 5?

    Equation: _____

    Solution: _____

Practice 33

Equations can often be written to make problem solving easier.

- What number is 5 times 30?

    $n = 5 \times 30$ so n = 150

- What number divided by 3 equals 6?

    $\frac{n}{3} = 6$ so $n = 18$

Directions: Write an equation for each word problem. Then solve the equation. The first one is done for you.

1. What number divided by 4 equals 10?

    Equation: _____$n/4 = 10$_____

    Solution: _____$n = 40$_____

2. What number times 11 equals 132?

    Equation: _____

    Solution: _____

3. What number divided by 11 equals 3?

    Equation: _____

    Solution: _____

4. What number divided into 44 that equals 11?

    Equation: _____

    Solution: _____

5. What number times 10 equals 50?

    Equation: _____

    Solution: _____

6. What number divided into 20 equals 2?

    Equation: _____

    Solution: _____

7. What is the length of a rectangle which has a width of 6 feet and an area of 72 square feet?

    Equation: _____

    Solution: _____

8. What is the width of a rectangle which has a length of 10 feet and an area of 80 square feet?

    Equation: _____

    Solution: _____

9. What number multiplied by itself equals 100?

    Equation: _____

    Solution: _____

10. What is the length of one side of a square which has an area of 64 square inches?

    Equation: _____

    Solution: _____

Practice 34 ꔷ ꔷ ꔷ ꔷ ꔷ ꔷ ꔷ ꔷ ꔷ ꔷ ꔷ ꔷ ꔷ ꔷ ꔷ

Experimental probability tells you what actually happens when you flip a coin or roll a die. Theoretical probability tells you what the mathematical chances are of an event happening.

What are the chances of flipping one penny and the coin landing on heads? There are two possibilities, heads or tails (1 chance in 2).

1. Flip a penny 50 times and record the results below.

   ____ ____ ____ ____ ____ ____ ____ ____

   ____ ____ ____ ____ ____ ____ ____ ____

   ____ ____ ____ ____ ____ ____ ____ ____

   ____ ____ ____ ____ ____ ____ ____ ____

   ____ ____ ____ ____ ____ ____ ____ ____

   ____ ____ ____ ____ ____ ____ ____ ____

   ____ ____

2. How many times did you flip heads? _____

3. Did you flip heads more or less than 1 in 2 times? (Did you flip heads more or less than 25 times?) _____

What are the chances of flipping two heads when flipping two pennies?

These are the 4 possibilities: (P = Possibility, H = Heads, T = Tails)

P1	P2		P1	P2		P1	P2		P1	P2
H	H		H	T		T	H		T	T

4. What are the chances of flipping two heads? _____

5. What are the chances of flipping two tails? _____

6. What are the chances of flipping 1 head and 1 tail? _____

7. Flip two pennies 48 times and record the results below.

   ____ ____ ____ ____ ____ ____ ____ ____

   ____ ____ ____ ____ ____ ____ ____ ____

   ____ ____ ____ ____ ____ ____ ____ ____

   ____ ____ ____ ____ ____ ____ ____ ____

   ____ ____ ____ ____ ____ ____ ____ ____

   ____ ____ ____ ____ ____ ____ ____ ____

8. How many times did you flip two heads? _____

9. How many times did you flip two tails? _____

10. How many times did you flip one head and one tail? _____

11. Did you flip two heads more or less than 1 in 4 times? (Did you flip two heads more or less than 12 times?) _____

Practice 35 ⟲ ⟲ ⟲ ⟲ ⟲ ⟲ ⟲ ⟲ ⟲ ⟲ ⟲ ⟲ ⟲ ⟲

Susan has three tops: 1 red, 1 green, and 1 blue. She has two skirts: 1 plaid and 1 striped. How many different combinations can she wear without repeating a combination? Make a chart.

> blue top + plaid skirt   green top + plaid skirt
>
> blue top + striped skirt   red top + striped skirt
>
> green top + striped skirt   red top + plaid skirt
>
> **Answer:** 6 different combinations

Directions: Make a chart to help you answer each of these combination word problems. If more space is needed, make an additional chart on a separate piece of paper.

1. The soccer coach has 3 different uniform tops: 1 red, 1 yellow, and 1 purple. She has 3 uniform shorts: 1 white, 1 black, and 1 brown. How many different combinations can she make?

Chart

red uniform top	+	white shorts		_____	+	_____
red uniform top	+	black shorts		_____	+	_____
red uniform top	+	brown shorts		_____	+	_____
_____	+	_____		_____	+	_____

Answer: _____

2. Christina has 5 blouses: white, purple, red, pink, and green. She has 3 jeans: black, blue, and brown. How many different combinations can she wear?

Chart

_____	+	_____		_____	+	_____
_____	+	_____		_____	+	_____
_____	+	_____		_____	+	_____
_____	+	_____		_____	+	_____

Answer: _____

3. The PTA offered sundaes with 3 choices of ice cream: chocolate, vanilla, and strawberry. There were 4 possible toppings: fudge, butterscotch, cherries, and nuts. How many combinations could you make using only one kind of ice cream and one choice of topping for each sundae?

Chart

_____	+	_____		_____	+	_____
_____	+	_____		_____	+	_____
_____	+	_____		_____	+	_____
_____	+	_____		_____	+	_____

Answer: _____

Practice 36 ꙮꙮꙮꙮꙮꙮꙮꙮꙮꙮꙮꙮꙮ

Directions: Coiffures 4 U is run by two enterprising fifth grade boys in their garage. You can get lawn mower flattops and weed cutter trims at very inexpensive prices and you always get a discount.

Help the customers compute how much they will save. The first one is done for you.

Reminder: Convert the percentage to a decimal and multiply.

1. Joey went into Coiffures 4 U to get a lawnmower flattop. The usual charge is $20 but he got a 30% discount. How much money did Joey save?

$20
x .30
$6.00

   Discount: ____$6.00____

2. James went into Coiffures 4 U to get a weed cutter trim. The usual charge is $15 but the boys gave him a 40% discount because he was a neighbor. How much money did he save?

   Discount: _____

3. Jordan decided to get a rotary mower trim. The usual fee is $40, but the boys decided to give him a deal because he was a good football player. Jordan got a 20% discount. How much did he save?

   Discount: _____

4. Allison went in for a leaf blower hairdo. The normal price is $90 because it takes so much time, but she got a 25% discount. How much did Allison save?

   Discount: _____

5. Joshua got a flattop and a weed cutter trim. The usual price for this combo is $27, but he got a 40% discount. How much did he save?

   Discount: _____

6. Serena asked for a leaf blower coiffure and a lawn mower trim to get rid of her split ends. The original charge for this was $100, but the boys gave her a 35% discount. How much did she save?

   Discount: _____

7. Michelle wanted a lawn mower trim for her pony tail. The usual price was $18 but the boys gave her a 40% discount. How much did she save?

   Discount: _____

8. Tom got a weed cutter super close trim. The usual price was $28 but he got a 30% discount. How much did he save?

   Discount: _____

Test Practice 1

Directions: Fill in the circle for the correct answer to each word problem.

1. One bag of gumballs weighs 9 ounces How many ounces do 22 bags of gumballs weigh?

   (A) 218 oz   (C) 198 ounces

   (B) 188 ounces   (D) 208 ounces

2. A European white birch grows 50 feet tall. A California redwood grows 325 feet tall. How much taller is the redwood?

   (A) 175 feet   (C) 225 feet

   (B) 275 feet   (D) 255 feet

3. Pete Rose had 14,053 at bats in the major leagues. Hank Aaron had 12,364 at bats. How many fewer at bats did Hank Aaron have?

   (A) 1,688   (C) 2,689

   (B) 1,679   (D) 1,689

4. A candy factory packages 20 chocolate balls in each box. How many boxes will it need to package 4,260 balls?

   (A) 213   (C) 2,213

   (B) 223   (D) 193

5. A school building has two wings. One wing is 194 feet long. The other wing is 229 feet long. What is the combined length of the two wings?

   (A) 444 feet   (C) 423 feet

   (B) 433 feet   (D) 2,243 feet

6. One school bus will seat 88 students. How many students can be seated in 29 school buses?

   (A) 2,552   (C) 3,552

   (B) 2,462   (D) 2,562

7. What is the difference between 45,009 and 32,997?

   (A) 13,212   (C) 12,012

   (B) 12,112   (D) 12,222

8. A toy company packs 25 marbles in one bag. How many bags will they need to pack 5,275 marbles?

   (A) 221   (C) 311

   (B) 211   (D) 271

9. Each person at a party will receive 24 ounces of soft drink. How many ounces will it take to serve 45 guests?

   (A) 1,280 ounces   (C) 9,800 ounces

   (B) 2,080 ounces   (D) 1,080 ounces

10. What is the sum of 12,344 and 98,765?

   (A) 111,109   (C) 211,119

   (B) 111,129   (D) 111,119

Test Practice 2

Directions: Fill in the circle for the correct answer to each word problem.

1. What is the sum of $1\frac{1}{3}$ and $2\frac{3}{8}$?

   (A) $2\frac{17}{24}$ (C) $3\frac{17}{24}$

   (B) $3\frac{4}{11}$ (D) $1\frac{1}{24}$

2. A green lacewing is 5/8 inches long. A large caddisfly is 15/16 inches long. How much

   (A) 6/16 inches   (C) 5/8 inches

   (B) 5/16 inches   (D) 1/4 inches

3. You ate 5/12 of 1 whole pizza. How much pizza was left?

   (A) 7/12   (C) 1/2

   (B) 6/12   (D) 3/4

4. A licorice stick $10\frac{1}{2}$ feet long is being cut evenly into pieces 3/4 of a foot long. How many 3/4 feet pieces can be cut?

   (A) 24   (C) 12

   (B) 16   (D) 14

5. The length of a piece of paper is 11 inches The width is $8\frac{1}{2}$ inches What is the difference?

   (A) $3\frac{1}{2}$ inches   (C) $2\frac{1}{2}$ inches

   (B) $1\frac{1}{2}$ inches   (D) $3\frac{1}{4}$ inches

6. A spotted ground squirrel weighs $4\frac{3}{8}$ ounces A Mexican ground squirrel weighs $11\frac{5}{8}$ ounces How much do they weigh altogether?

   (A) $15\frac{7}{8}$ ounces   (C) $15\frac{1}{4}$ ounces

   (B) 16 ounces   (D) $11\frac{1}{8}$ ounces

7. A Chew Rite candy bar weighs $3\frac{2}{3}$ ounces What is the weight of 33 Chew Rite candy bars?

   (A) 221 ounces   (C) 121 ounces

   (B) 101 ounces   (D) $36\frac{2}{3}$ ounces

8. A cup of cola holds $8\frac{1}{2}$ ounces How many cups can you pour from a container holding 102 ounces

   (A) 14   (C) 10

   (B) 22   (D) 12

9. What is the product of $2\frac{1}{2}$ and $9\frac{1}{5}$?

   (A) 28   (C) 23

   (B) $11\frac{3}{8}$ (D) $117\frac{3}{8}$

10. A bee assassin is 5/8 inches long. How many bee assassins are in a line $7\frac{1}{2}$ inches long?

    (A) 20   (C) 13

    (B) 13   (D) 11

Test Practice 3

Directions: Fill in the circle for the correct answer to each word problem.

1. Jimmy had $45.98 in his wallet and $39.76 in his piggy bank. How much money did he have altogether?
   - (A) $86.74
   - (B) $85.76
   - (C) $95.74
   - (D) $85.74

2. A box of candy sells for $5.69. How much will it cost for 50 boxes of candy?
   - (A) $280.50
   - (B) $284.50
   - (C) $384.50
   - (D) $184.50

3. A mourning dove weighs 4.2 ounces. How much do 23 doves weigh?
   - (A) 86.6 ounces
   - (B) 96.4 ounces
   - (C) 96.6 ounces
   - (D) 94.6 ounces

4. A line of 9 footballs touching end to end measures 256.5 centimeters long. How long is each football?
   - (A) 30.4 centimeters
   - (B) 29.5 centimeters
   - (C) 280.5 centimeters
   - (D) 28.5 centimeters

5. A regular bottle of Squeaky Clean Soap holds 7.56 ounces. The extra large size holds 15.4 ounces. How much more soap does the extra large bottle hold?
   - (A) 7.74 ounces
   - (B) 8.64 ounces
   - (C) 6.84 ounces
   - (D) 7.84 ounces

6. The Anywhere House received $199.20 on the sale of 20 albums by Hill Billy Hank. What was the cost of each album?
   - (A) $9.96
   - (B) $10.86
   - (C) $99.60
   - (D) $9.86

7. The monarch butterfly has a wingspan of 10.2 centimeters. The queen Butterfly has a wingspan of 8.6 centimeters. How much wider is the monarch wingspan?
   - (A) 2.6 centimeters
   - (B) 1.6 centimeters
   - (C) 18.8 centimeters
   - (D) 2.4 centimeters

8. A sports shop sold 13 Rough Rider Mountain Bikes for a total of $1,948.44. How much did each bike cost?
   - (A) $159.78
   - (B) $148.88
   - (C) $149.98
   - (D) $149.88

9. What is the quotient of 107.8 divided by 11?
   - (A) 98
   - (B) .98
   - (C) 9.8
   - (D) 12

10. What is the sum of 1.246 and 23.6?
    - (A) 248.46
    - (B) 24.846
    - (C) 148.2
    - (D) 2,484.6

 #3730 Practice Makes Perfect: Word Problems

Test Practice 4 ༄ ✺ ༄ ✺ ✺ ༄ ✺ ༄ ✺ ✺ ༄ ༄ ✺

Directions: Fill in the circle for the correct answer to each word problem.

1. How many degrees does angle *x* represent?

Ⓐ 60°
Ⓑ 120°
Ⓒ 40°
Ⓓ 80°

6. How many degrees are represented by angle *x* in the triangle below?

Ⓐ 45°
Ⓑ 90°
Ⓒ 30°
Ⓓ 135°

---

2. What is the perimeter of this rectangle?

Ⓐ 35 centimeters
Ⓑ 135 centimeters
Ⓒ 70 centimeters
Ⓓ 286 centimeters

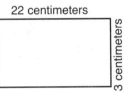

7. How many degrees are represented by angle *x*?

Ⓐ 35°
Ⓑ 65°
Ⓒ 55°
Ⓓ 45°

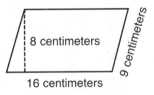

---

3. What is the area of the figure shown above?

Ⓐ 90 sq. centimeters
Ⓑ 296 sq. centimeters
Ⓒ 286 sq. centimeters
Ⓓ 936 sq. centimeters

8. What is the perimeter of this parallelogram?

Ⓐ 25 centimeters
Ⓑ 48 centimeters
Ⓒ 50 centimeters
Ⓓ 24 centimeters

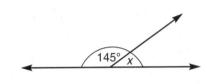

---

4. What is the total number of degrees in the three interior angles of any triangle?

Ⓐ 360°
Ⓑ 80°
Ⓒ 160°
Ⓓ 180°

9. What is the area of the parallelogram above?

Ⓐ 128 sq. centimeters
Ⓑ 144 sq. centimeters
Ⓒ 48 sq. centimeters
Ⓓ 136 sq. centimeters

---

5. What is the perimeter of a square which is 15 inches long on each side?

Ⓐ 225 inches
Ⓑ 60 inches
Ⓒ 600 inches
Ⓓ 90 inches

10. What is the area of a rectangle which is 9 feet long and 6 feet wide?

Ⓐ 30 sq. feet
Ⓑ 56 sq. feet
Ⓒ 15 sq. feet
Ⓓ 54 sq. feet

Test Practice 5

Directions: Fill in the circle for the correct answer to each word problem.

1. The Anywhere House sold the latest album by Guess Who for $17.96. How much money did they receive on the sale of 44 of these albums?

    (A) $780.24   (C) $790.34

    (B) $724.90   (D) $790.24

2. Rosa bought a sweater which was originally priced at $38. She received a 30% discount. How much money did she save?

    (A) $12.00   (C) $11.40

    (B) $12.40   (D) $3.80

3. The cafeteria manager gets sandwich rolls which are 150 inches long. Each student receives a 6-inch roll. How many students can the manager feed with one long roll?

    (A) 25   (C) 35

    (B) 205   (D) 144

4. A green skipper butterfly has a wingspan of $1\frac{3}{8}$ inches The pine white butterfly has a wingspan of 2 inches How much wider is the pine white?

    (A) 3/8 inches   (C) $1\frac{3}{8}$ inches

    (B) 3/4 inches   (D) 5/8 inches

5. A grizzly bear weighs 1,496 lbs. The polar bear weighs 1,100 lbs. How much heavier is the grizzly bear?

    (A) 296 lbs.   (C) 2,596 lbs.

    (B) 396 lbs.   (D) 496 lbs.

6. What is the area of a football playing field which is 160 feet wide and 300 feet long?

    (A) 40,000 sq. feet   (C) 48,800 sq. feet

    (B) 49,000 sq. feet   (D) 48,000 sq. feet

7. What is the product of 18.9 and 3.46?

    (A) 65.394   (C) 56.394

    (B) 66.394   (D) 66.494

8. Karen needs to cut a wire $10\frac{1}{2}$ feet long into pieces which are 1/2 feet long. How many 1/2 feet pieces can she cut?

    (A) $10\frac{1}{2}$ (C) 20

    (B) 22   (D) 21

9. What is the perimeter of an equilateral triangle which is 9.3 meters long on each side?

    (A) 2.79 meters   (C) 27.9 meters

    (B) 0.279 meters   (D) 279 meters

10. Compute the sum of 1.539 and 34.98.

    (A) 50.37   (C) 49.27

    (B) 3.6519   (D) 36.519

 #3730 Practice Makes Perfect: Word Problems

Test Practice 6 ⟋ ⟍ ⟋ ⟍ ⟋ ⟍ ⟋ ⟍ ⟋ ⟍ ⟋ ⟋ ⟍

Directions: Fill in the circle for the correct answer to each word problem.

1. The science teacher gave each of the 30 students in his class 2.75 ounces of vinegar. How much vinegar did he use for all 30 students?

   (A) 82 ounces   (C) 82.5 ounces

   (B) 72.5 ounces   (D) 802.5 ounces

2. Melanie had to read a book which was 465 pages long in 15 days. How many pages did she need to read each night?

   (A) 31   (C) 33

   (B) 21   (D) 30

3. Families use 24 billion gallons of water each day in the United States. How many billion gallons do they use in 1 year? (There are 365 days in 1 year.)

   (A) 8,760 billion gallons

   (B) 8,660 billion gallons

   (C) 8,880 billion gallons

   (D) 9,760 billion gallons

4. Rhode Island has an area of 1,545 sq. miles. Texas has an area of 268,601 sq. miles. How many more square miles are in Texas?

   (A) 266,656 sq. miles

   (B) 260,556 sq. miles

   (C) 267,056 sq. miles

   (D) 270,146 sq. miles

5. A California katydid is $2\frac{3}{8}$ inches long. A house cricket is 3/4 inches long. How much longer is the katydid?

   (A) $1\frac{2}{8}$ inches   (C) $1\frac{3}{8}$ inches

   (B) $2\frac{3}{8}$ inches   (D) $1\frac{3}{8}$ inches

6. A male black widow spider is 1/8 inches long. How many of these spiders could sit in a line $4\frac{1}{2}$ inches long?

   (A) 31   (C) 39

   (B) 35   (D) 36

7. It is 2,786 miles from New York to Los Angeles and 2,934 miles from New York to San Francisco. How much farther is it from New York to San Francisco?

   (A) 248 miles   (C) 158 miles

   (B) 48 miles   (D) 148 miles

8. What is the difference between 33,568 and 19,979?

   (A) 13,399   (C) 13,589

   (B) 15,589   (D) 23,589

9. The population of New York City is 8,008,278. The population of Newark, New Jersey, is 273,546. What is the total?

   (A) 7,734,732   (C) 8,281,824

   (B) 8,381,824   (D) 8,281,934

10. What is the product of 0.91 and 200?

    (A) 192   (C) 282

    (B) 182   (D) 192

Answer Sheet

Test Practice 1	Test Practice 2	Test Practice 3
1. Ⓐ Ⓑ Ⓒ Ⓓ	1. Ⓐ Ⓑ Ⓒ Ⓓ	1. Ⓐ Ⓑ Ⓒ Ⓓ
2. Ⓐ Ⓑ Ⓒ Ⓓ	2. Ⓐ Ⓑ Ⓒ Ⓓ	2. Ⓐ Ⓑ Ⓒ Ⓓ
3. Ⓐ Ⓑ Ⓒ Ⓓ	3. Ⓐ Ⓑ Ⓒ Ⓓ	3. Ⓐ Ⓑ Ⓒ Ⓓ
4. Ⓐ Ⓑ Ⓒ Ⓓ	4. Ⓐ Ⓑ Ⓒ Ⓓ	4. Ⓐ Ⓑ Ⓒ Ⓓ
5. Ⓐ Ⓑ Ⓒ Ⓓ	5. Ⓐ Ⓑ Ⓒ Ⓓ	5. Ⓐ Ⓑ Ⓒ Ⓓ
6. Ⓐ Ⓑ Ⓒ Ⓓ	6. Ⓐ Ⓑ Ⓒ Ⓓ	6. Ⓐ Ⓑ Ⓒ Ⓓ
7. Ⓐ Ⓑ Ⓒ Ⓓ	7. Ⓐ Ⓑ Ⓒ Ⓓ	7. Ⓐ Ⓑ Ⓒ Ⓓ
8. Ⓐ Ⓑ Ⓒ Ⓓ	8. Ⓐ Ⓑ Ⓒ Ⓓ	8. Ⓐ Ⓑ Ⓒ Ⓓ
9. Ⓐ Ⓑ Ⓒ Ⓓ	9. Ⓐ Ⓑ Ⓒ Ⓓ	9. Ⓐ Ⓑ Ⓒ Ⓓ
10. Ⓐ Ⓑ Ⓒ Ⓓ	10. Ⓐ Ⓑ Ⓒ Ⓓ	10. Ⓐ Ⓑ Ⓒ Ⓓ

Test Practice 4	Test Practice 5	Test Practice 6
1. Ⓐ Ⓑ Ⓒ Ⓓ	1. Ⓐ Ⓑ Ⓒ Ⓓ	1. Ⓐ Ⓑ Ⓒ Ⓓ
2. Ⓐ Ⓑ Ⓒ Ⓓ	2. Ⓐ Ⓑ Ⓒ Ⓓ	2. Ⓐ Ⓑ Ⓒ Ⓓ
3. Ⓐ Ⓑ Ⓒ Ⓓ	3. Ⓐ Ⓑ Ⓒ Ⓓ	3. Ⓐ Ⓑ Ⓒ Ⓓ
4. Ⓐ Ⓑ Ⓒ Ⓓ	4. Ⓐ Ⓑ Ⓒ Ⓓ	4. Ⓐ Ⓑ Ⓒ Ⓓ
5. Ⓐ Ⓑ Ⓒ Ⓓ	5. Ⓐ Ⓑ Ⓒ Ⓓ	5. Ⓐ Ⓑ Ⓒ Ⓓ
6. Ⓐ Ⓑ Ⓒ Ⓓ	6. Ⓐ Ⓑ Ⓒ Ⓓ	6. Ⓐ Ⓑ Ⓒ Ⓓ
7. Ⓐ Ⓑ Ⓒ Ⓓ	7. Ⓐ Ⓑ Ⓒ Ⓓ	7. Ⓐ Ⓑ Ⓒ Ⓓ
8. Ⓐ Ⓑ Ⓒ Ⓓ	8. Ⓐ Ⓑ Ⓒ Ⓓ	8. Ⓐ Ⓑ Ⓒ Ⓓ
9. Ⓐ Ⓑ Ⓒ Ⓓ	9. Ⓐ Ⓑ Ⓒ Ⓓ	9. Ⓐ Ⓑ Ⓒ Ⓓ
10. Ⓐ Ⓑ Ⓒ Ⓓ	10. Ⓐ Ⓑ Ⓒ Ⓓ	10. Ⓐ Ⓑ Ⓒ Ⓓ

Answer Key @ @ @ @ @ @ @ @ @ @ @ @

Page 4
1. how many pages left to read; 72 pages
2. how many pages read in 7 nights, 140 pages
3. how many minutes the bike was ridden; 95 minutes
4. how many coins I have; 54 coins
5. how many marbles your friend has; 112 marbles
6. how many candies each player received; 9 candies
7. how many more shots were made; 6 shots

Page 5
1. subtraction; 19 fifth graders
2. multiplication; $1,560.00
3. multiplication; 540 textbooks
4. addition; 401 students
5. multiplication; 2,012 cookies
6. division; 23 candy bars
7. multiplication; $872.00

Page 6
1. subtraction; 15 points
2. subtraction; 26 third graders
3. subtraction; 12 points
4. subtraction; $2.51
5. addition; 1,277 students
6. addition; 1,651 candy boxes

Page 7
1. multiplication; 296 cards
2. division; 26 candies
3. multiplication; $2.00
4. multiplication; 1,564
5. division; 13
6. multiplication, $9.00
7. addition and division; 20 points
8. multiplication; 320 sq. feet

Page 8
1. addition; $133.16
2. subtraction; 48 minutes
3. multiplication; 301 lbs.
4. division; 84 pages
5. division; 310 miles
6. subtraction; 167 cards
7. addition; 207 minutes
8. subtraction; 103 minutes
9. division; $5.56

10. multiplication; $30

Page 9
1. 300 balls
2. $11.13
3. $6.21
4. $209.24
5. 15,600 cards
6. $33.16
7. 510 toys
8. 134 marbles
9. 120 marbles

Page 10
1. 5,000 lollipops
2. 506 boxes
3. 6,544 suckers
4. 10,703 chocolates
5. 1,881 gumballs
6. 15,509 gumballs
7. 76,567 squirters
8. 611 boxes
9. 15,000 gumballs
10. 100,656 suckers

Page 11
1. 8; 3/8   6. 24; 7/24
2. 6; 1/2   7. 12; 1/12
3. 6; 1/6   8. 24; 11/24
4. 12; 5/12   9. 12; 1/12
5. 8; 1/8   10. 24; 5/24

Page 12
1. 1 1/4 lb. beans
   3/4 lb. hamburger
   1 lb. tomatoes
   1/2 lb. macaroni
   1 ounces chili pepper
   1 1/2 ounces hot sauce
   5 ounces tomato sauce
   4 ounces water
2. 1 2/3 lb. beans
   1 lb. hamburger
   1 1/3 lb. tomatoes
   2/3 lb. macaroni
   1 1/3 ounces chili pepper
   2 ounces hot sauce
   6 2/3 ounces tomato sauce
   5 1/3 ounces water
3. 2 1/2 lb. beans
   1 1/2 lb. hamburger
   2 lb. tomatoes
   1 lb. macaroni
   2 ounces chili pepper
   3 ounces hot sauce
   10 ounces tomato sauce
   8 ounces water
4. 10 bags
5. 6 sacks
6. 3 boxes
7. 6 trays

Page 13
1. 5 qt.
2. 2/3 qt.
3. 1/16 gal.
4. 1/9 gal.
5. 20 qt.
6. 1/12 qt.
7. 1/18 qt.
8. 19/24 qt.
9. 18 sweet peas
10. 1/12 gal.

Page 14
1. 1/16 inches
2. 7/8 inches
3. 1/8 inches
4. 18 beetles
5. 12 inches
6. 62 billbugs
7. 9/16 inches
8. 1 1/8 inches
9. 39 boll weevils
10. 20 inches

Page 15
1. 3 3/4 inches
2. 4 3/4 inches
3. 3/4 inches
4. 1 1/2 inches
5. 5 5/8 inches
6. 2 3/4 inches
7. 6 5/8 inches
8. 2 7/8 inches
9. 10 1/8 inches
10. 8 3/4 inches

Page 16
1. 1 1/2 mi.
2. 1 1/2 minches
3. 1 1/3 mi.
4. 50 minches
5. 2 1/3 minches
6. 8 3/4 mi.
7. 3/4 blocks
8. 54 blocks
9. 1/2 block
10. 2 1/2 mi.

Page 17
1. 27 5/6 inches
2. 1 7/15 ounces
3. 1/2 ounces
4. 36 inches
5. 2 3/8 feet
6. 1 1/6 inches
7. 5/16 ounces
8. 1/4 feet
9. 20 ounces
10. 18 2/3 gal.

Page 18
1. 1/4 inches
2. 3/8 inches
3. 6 3/4 inches
4. 20 inches
5. 9/16 inches
6. 33 inches
7. 1/2 inches
8. 70 spiders
9. 7 1/2 inches
10. 2 47/64 inches

Page 19
1. $3.10   6. $18.95
2. $209.70   7. $7.12
3. $5.72   8. $1,160.12
4. 41 CDs   9. $1,418.97
5. $598   10. $19.08

Page 20
1. $0.46
2. $5.20
3. $30
4. 14 super sundaes
5. $5.83
6. $29.80
7. 20 large sundaes
8. $4.87
9. $63
10. $0.90

Page 21
1. $4.24   6. $15.75
2. $1.24   7. $67.50
3. $8.51   8. $44.85
4. $4.10   9. $4.94
5. $7.23   10. $12.96

Page 22
1. $20.93   6. $4.10
2. $16.01   7. $8.74
3. $14.95   8. $6.01
4. $29.25   9. $85.05
5. $12.98   10. $17.95

Page 23
1. 3.6 centimeters
2. 5.6 centimeters
3. 195.96 centimeters
4. 171.8 centimeters
5. 340.54 centimeters
6. 177.9 centimeters
7. 71.21 centimeters
8. 331.4 centimeters
9. 26.91 centimeters
10. 430.21 centimeters

Page 24
1. 0.54 kg   6. 96.075 kg
2. 28 ounces 7. 45 kg
3. 28.8 lbs.   8. 3.08 kg
4. 111 lbs.   9. 5.5 ounces
5. 26.1 kg   10. 77.5 lbs.

Answer Key (cont.) ⟋ ◉ ⟋ ◉ ⟋ ◉ ⟋ ◉ ⟋ ◉ ⟋

Page 25
1. 21.05 meters
2. 5.42 ounces
3. $17.43
4. 4.26 ounces
5. 20.4 feet
6. 4.31 ounces
7. 56.39 feet
8. 2.09 grams
9. 9.96 ounces
10. 0.8878 mi.
11. 0.678223 ounces

Page 26
1. California
2. Minnesota/ Maryland
3. Illinois/ Pennsylvania
4. Michigan
5. 15
6. 20
7. New York
8. 5th
9. 7th
10. 8th
11. 6th
12. 8th
13. 6th
14. 7th

Page 27
1. 35 years
2. 30 years
3. United States/1900
4. 47 years
5. 1750
6. 20th (1900–2000)
7. 2250 years
8. 2001
9. 1993
10. 1997/1998
11. 1994
12. 1992
13. 1994/1998–2001
14. 1992/1995/1996/1997
15. National League

Page 28
1. 50
2. 10
3. 25
4. 45
5. soccer/ basketball
6. swimming/ bicycling
7. 45
8. 20
9. 25
10. 2
11. 2
12. yes - 1
13. 2
14. 3
15. 8
16. 196

Page 29
1. Checkers
2. Old Maid
3. 6
4. 6
5. 6
6. Solitaire/Twenty-One
7. 49
8. 23
9. 23 inches
10. 60 inches
11. bald eagle
12. sparrow hawk
13. 24 inches
14. 6 inches

Page 30
1. 38 feet
2. 45 feet
3. 52 meters
4. 48 meters
5. 21 meters
6. 40 meters
7. 43 feet
8. 56 meters

Page 31
1. 135 sq. feet
2. 72 sq. feet
3. 24 sq. feet
4. 136 sq. feet
5. 192 sq. feet
6. 72 sq. feet
7. 320 sq. feet
8. 169 sq. feet

Page 32
1. 120°
2. 50°
3. 110°
4. 30°
5. 60°
6. 45°
7. 80°
8. 55°

Page 33
1. 60°
2. 45°
3. 70°
4. 50°
5. 30°
6. 10°
7. 40°
8. 25°

Page 34
1. mall
2. school
3. bank
4. III
5. I
6. (3, ⁻8)
7. library
8. (2, 3)
9. park
10. IV

Page 35
1. $n = 20 - 7$
   $n = 13$
2. $n = 30 - 13$
   $n = 17$
3. $n + 9 = 15$
   $n = 6$
4. $n = 29 + 4$
   $n = 33$
5. $n - 14 = 29$
   $n = 43$
6. $n + 23 = 30$
   $n = 7$
7. $n + 22 = 40$
   $n = 18$
8. $60 - 22 = n$
   $n = 38$
9. $25 + n = 61$
   $n = 36$
10. $n + 16 = 40 + 5$
    $n = 29$

Page 36
1. $n/4 = 10$
   $n = 40$
2. $n \times 11 = 132$
   $n = 12$
3. $n/11 = 3$
   $n = 33$
4. $44/n = 11$
   $n = 4$
5. $n \times 10 = 50$
   $n = 5$
6. $20/n = 2$
   $n = 10$
7. $n = 72/6$
   $n = 12$ feet
8. $n = 80/10$
   $n = 8$ feet
9. $n \times n = 100$
   $n = 10$
10. $n \times n = 64$
    $n = 8$

Page 37
1.–3. Answers will vary.
4. 1 in 4
5. 1 in 4
6. 1 in 2 or 2 in 4
7.–11. Answers will vary.

Page 38
1. red top + white shorts
   red top + black shorts
   red top + brown shorts
   yellow top + white shorts
   yellow top + black shorts
   yellow top + brown shorts
   purple top + white shorts
   purple top + black shorts
   purple top + brown shorts
   9 combinations
2. white blouse + black jeans
   white blouse + blue jeans
   white blouse + brown jeans
   purple blouse + black jeans
   purple blouse + blue jeans
   purple blouse + brown jeans
   red blouse + black jeans
   red blouse + blue jeans
   red blouse + brown jeans
   pink blouse + black jeans
   pink blouse + blue jeans
   pink blouse + brown jeans
   green blouse + black jeans
   green blouse + blue jeans
   green blouse + brown jeans
   15 combinations
3. chocolate + fudge
   chocolate + butterscotch
   chocolate + cherries
   chocolate + nuts
   vanilla + fudge
   vanilla + butterscotch
   vanilla + cherries
   vanilla + nuts
   strawberry + fudge
   strawberry + butterscotch
   strawberry + cherries
   strawberry + nuts
   12 combinations
4. multiplication

Page 39
1. $6.00
2. $6.00
3. $8.00
4. $22.50
5. $10.80
6. $35.00
7. $7.20
8. $8.40

Page 40
1. C
2. B
3. D
4. A
5. C
6. A
7. C
8. B
9. D
10. A

Page 41
1. C
2. B
3. A
4. D
5. C
6. B
7. C
8. D
9. C
10. C

Page 42
1. D
2. B
3. C
4. D
5. D
6. A
7. B
8. D
9. C
10. B

Page 43
1. A
2. C
3. C
4. D
5. B
6. A
7. A
8. C
9. A
10. D

Page 44
1. D
2. C
3. A
4. D
5. B
6. D
7. A
8. D
9. C
10. D

Page 45
1. C
2. A
3. A
4. C
5. D
6. D
7. D
8. C
9. C
10. B